Covert Operations in World War II: The Histo Most Daring Secret Missions

By Charles River Editors

A B2 radio set

About Charles River Editors

Charles River Editors is a boutique digital publishing company, specializing in bringing history back to life with educational and engaging books on a wide range of topics. Keep up to date with our new and free offerings with this 5 second sign up on our weekly mailing list, and visit Our Kindle Author Page to see other recently published Kindle titles.

We make these books for you and always want to know our readers' opinions, so we encourage you to leave reviews and look forward to publishing new and exciting titles each week.

Introduction

Resistance fighters in 1944

Covert Operations in World War II

When people think about the Second World War, they seldom think in terms of silence and small acts. This was a war in which the industry of entire nations was rearranged to feed fighting, and it was fought on a scale in which battles could include hundreds of thousands of combatants. Whole cities and populations were destroyed, with millions of casualties occurring at places like Leningrad.

But World War II was also a conflict in which modern covert operations first hit their stride. From the jungles of Burma to the streets of Paris, spies, saboteurs, and commandos carried out missions built on secrecy and cunning. Precise, self-contained operations could be as important to the outcome of the war as acts of massive destruction, whether it involved targeted assassinations, sabotaging key logistics, or counterintelligence to break up the enemy's own rings.

At the time, most of these operations were hidden from the public since that was the only way they could be successfully carried out, but in the years since, stories about various missions have emerged. They paint a picture of incredible courage and ingenuity, whether in war zones, enemy territory, or far from the front lines.

Covert Operations in World War II: The History and Legacy of the War's Most Daring Secret Missions chronicles some of the most daring operations carried out during the war. Along with pictures depicting important people, places, and events, you will learn about covert operations in World War II like never before.

Covert Operations in World War II: The History and Legacy of the War's Most Daring Secret Missions

About Charles River Editors

Introduction

   The Special Operations Executive

   The Office of Strategic Services

   Backroom Work

   Escape Operations

   Codes

   Vive la France

   Commando Raids

   The Balkans

   Asian Operations

   D-Day

   Germany's Covert Operations

   Italian Infiltrators

   Assassins and Politicians

   Undermining the Enemy

   Online Resources

   Further Reading

Free Books by Charles River Editors

Discounted Books by Charles River Editors

The Special Operations Executive

In the summer of 1940, conditions looked bleak for Great Britain as German troops expanded across Europe in a tidal wave of destruction. In September 1939, they had invaded Poland, conquering the nation in mere weeks and triggering the Second World War. The following spring, they had invaded Belgium, France, and the Netherlands and decisively defeated the armies of Britain and France, two of the world's supposed superpowers. Britain was the only independent nation still standing against the menace of Nazism, a haven for fugitive soldiers and place where the armies of a free Europe regrouped to consider what desperate measures it would take to fight back.

By July, Hugh Dalton, the minister of economic warfare, was working on an idea for a new approach to the war. Building on the examples of Chinese guerrillas, Irish revolutionaries, and the Spanish peasant soldiers who had defied Napoleon, he wanted to create a movement in enemy-occupied territory that would use sabotage, propaganda, political agitation, and terrorism to weaken the enemy. A new organization would be needed to encourage and support this cause. Following a meeting between Dalton and Prime Minister Winston Churchill on the 16th of July, this organization was founded under Dalton's oversight and christened the Special Operations Executive (SOE).

Lord Dalton

Dalton wanted the SOE to be a civil rather than a military organization, but he knew he would need to find military men to lead many of its operations. He started by recruiting Brigadier Colin Gubbins, an expert in guerrilla combat, as director of operations and training.

Sir Gubbins

The SOE faced the enormous challenge of building an unprecedented network of covert operatives practically from scratch. This was made more difficult by resistance within the British government, where several senior men, including Sir Charles Portal, chief of the air staff, opposed the use of the tactics Dalton had proposed. Other branches of the military also resented the priority given to the SOE, which had received scarce resources such as plastic explosives.

Recruitment was a tricky business, as the organization could not be open about its purpose or the sort of people it needed. Recruiters started by seeking out those with language skills and seeing if they fit the bill in other ways. Even before joining the SOE, recruits experienced clandestine meetings in restaurants and anonymous offices. Women were recruited as well as men. The First-Aid Nursing Yeomanry (FANY), an all-female volunteer organization, provided some of the support staff and helped with recruitment by encouraging men to impress attractive young ladies by committing to the cause.

Naturally, recruitment on the continent was more difficult. It started with the introduction of agents in Poland on the 15th of February, 1941. It was easiest to start in Poland, as it already had a resistance movement in place and many Polish soldiers had escaped to Britain after the fall of their country, making them ideal agents.

In the early days, the SOE staff had worked around the clock building up their new organization. Recruits were trained in unarmed combat, resisting interrogation, parachute landings, and a host of other specialist skills they would need. They were taught lock-breaking by a burglar, disguise by an actor, and had to undergo rigorous survival and fitness training. Their discretion was tested by approaches from attractive women.

Within months, the SOE had its own training regimes, bases of operation, tests, and hierarchy. It had the men and women ready to go into action. Now it was time, as Churchill had put it, to set Europe ablaze.

In the early days, the SOE was unable to obtain ships and planes from elsewhere in the British services. The resources were needed for keeping up the war effort, and the new branch of government had yet to prove it was worth diverting resources from other services for, so the SOE recruited its own small fleet under Lieutenant Commander Gerald Holdsworth. Mostly made up of fishing vessels from Brittany with French crews, the fleet worked out of the Helford River in Cornwall, making dangerous night-time expeditions across the Channel.

The Helford Flotillas had a number of tasks. They dropped off agents in France as the SOE made its first attempts to build up a network on the continent. They also provided supplies for the French Resistance, whom the British had encouraged to grow as they tried to establish connections with them. They brought out intelligence, bundles of papers provided by those gathering information behind German lines. They even smuggled people out of occupied Europe—refugees, escapees, and those with information important to the cause.

The Helford Flotillas' work was extremely difficult and dangerous. They had to negotiate the currents and rock formations of the French coast, requiring the recruitment of men with local knowledge. Naturally, they also had to evade detection by the Germans. Groups came ashore in small boats, carried out their work, and then signaled to the main craft for retrieval. It wasn't uncommon for landing parties to be left isolated in enemy territory after their boat had fled from German naval patrols.

In May 1941, the SOE began parachuting agents into France to work on building up the resistance. Everything they took with them was carefully examined to make sure it would blend in, right down to the fillings in their teeth, which were done differently in Britain than in France. Similar drops were made to send men and equipment into Scandinavia, where they joined the Norwegian and Danish resistance. A squadron of Halifax bombers, led by Squadron Leader Lewis Hodges, became specialists in making these drops and charting out courses to avoid anti-aircraft fire and German night fighters. The pilots were kept separate from the agents without even the chance to talk with them once they had boarded the plane.

Encouraging the resistance was not a simple matter of meeting up with existing networks. Many early operatives would have to recruit resistance groups almost from scratch, trying to identify idealistic and courageous locals who could be persuaded to join covert operations against the Germans. Later, radio operators were dropped in with wireless sets to connect resistance cells to the SOE in Britain.

Parachute drops had to take place at night. The flight of Allied planes over occupied territory drew attention, so the agents had to quickly bury their parachutes and get out of the area. The first agent to do this had to get away on his own, but later agents were assisted by welcoming committees from the resistance that arranged transport and safe houses for the operatives.

The second SOE agent to land in France, Pierre de Vomécourt, was captured just months after landing. His ignorance of the tiny details of life in occupied France had given him away in a local café, and he was eventually lured by a woman working as a German agent. It was far from the last time an infiltration would end badly. Entire groups of agents were sometimes captured by watchful local authorities or traps set for them by German intelligence. Perhaps most notably, Villa de Bois, an important safe house in Marseilles, was discovered by the Gestapo and used to capture numerous British agents.

As the war went on, ways of transporting agents became more sophisticated. Single-engine Lysander light aircraft and Hudson light bombers started landing behind enemy lines, dropping off and picking up agents. This avoided some of the danger and uncertainty of a parachute drop and allowed materials to be taken out, as was the case when the Polish resistance had provided examples of wreckage from German experiments in rocket building. All the while, many of the dangers for agents remained the same, including capture, torture, and imprisonment at the hands of the Reich.

Paul Maritz's picture of a Lysander MkIII

The Office of Strategic Services

Like the British, the Americans did not have a covert operations organization when they joined the war. Also like the British, it took them some time to realize it could be a powerful tool, so on the 13th of June in 1942, six months after the attack on Pearl Harbor, the Office of Strategic Services (OSS) was born.

The OSS was led by William "Wild Bill" Donovan. A highly decorated veteran and prominent lawyer, Donovan was full of energy and inspiration, and his leadership was crucial to building up the OSS in the face of serious opposition. Voices within the Pentagon, State Department, and White House all opposed the establishment of this new and untested organization that would carry out activities normally considered unacceptable, so Donovan had to fight for the very existence of the organization, battling through layers of bureaucracy to get the resources he needed and ensure the OSS's independence of action. He also worked hard to justify the use of covert tactics in warfare, citing precedents that stretched back to the Bible.

Donovan

A picture of Donovan reviewing members of the group in 1945

Donovan's work led to the growth of the OSS into an organization with over 13,000 staff and 40 offices scattered across the world. Its purposes were initially similar to that of SOE, including espionage, sabotage, and intelligence assessments, but with time and experience, it expanded to include economic, psychological, and guerrilla warfare, as well as counter-intelligence work.

From the start, the OSS and SOE sought to collaborate in their work. The SOE had concerns the political and bureaucratic mess around OSS would hold the American organization back, and they hoped to help their colleagues overcome these obstacles. They recognized that American resentment at Britain's leading role in the war could cause divisions and hinder trans-Atlantic cooperation, as had happened when the armies had been brought together in North Africa, and they were keen to avoid this happening in the field of clandestine warfare.

Working in their favor was the fact that the organization and recruitment techniques of the OSS were similar to those of the SOE. That said, recruitment included an element of bluntness that was at odds with the British approach, as all recruits were asked if they would be willing to land by parachute behind enemy lines, knowing that if they were caught they would be tortured to death. The OSS wanted to be sure of the character of its recruits from the start.

With its large immigrant communities, America provided access to recruits from a wide range of backgrounds, which meant they had a variety of languages and diverse knowledge of European customs. One large pool of recruits was the Italian American community, which had provided tough men, some of them from criminal gangs, who were keen to get put into action in fascist Italy.

The training was also similar to that in Britain. They were taught to kill with their bare hands and use a wide range of weapons, infuriating members of the Congressional Country Club when they ruined its golf course with hand grenade practice. There was training in parachuting, stealthy movement, and lock picking. They practiced for a host of different scenarios, from stealthily killing a sentry to drawing conclusions about the inhabitants of a room based on its contents.

The lives of these agents were absolutely secret. Even while training, friends and family had no idea where they were or what they were doing. This was the nature of the sort of war for which the OSS was preparing, a war in which secrecy was vital and deception was the only true defense.

OSS agents carried out their operations in two different formats. Some individual agents went in wearing civilian clothing, disguised and undercover behind enemy lines, while operational groups went in wearing uniforms, dressed and equipped as American soldiers. Their operations were more connected to guerrilla warfare than espionage, and so they worked by remaining hidden rather than blending in. Being in uniform meant they should, in theory at least, be treated as combatants if they were to be captured, thereby receiving protections intended for prisoners of war under the Geneva Convention.

Individual agents were sent into many different countries, and though most targets were enemy nations or occupied territories, there were also operations on neutral ground. Agents based out of the American embassy set up networks of operatives in Spain, then led by Franco's right-wing dictatorship, which remained neutral. Agents in Spain were important because of that country's sympathies to the Axis cause, and because many escaped POWs and downed airmen had been smuggled out through there via French escape lines.

Covert networks were often set up not as groups where everyone knew each other, but as chains of people. Thus, each person in the chain would know the person they had recruited and the person who had recruited them, but no one else. That way, if one person was captured, their interrogation would only put two others at immediate risk.

To oversee their work in Europe, the OSS set up a base in London, close to the American embassy. There, they had easier access to the continent and the leaders of the war in Europe. Donovan himself came across the Atlantic to try to persuade the American military and the British establishment to make use of the OSS and to allow it the freedom to operate, but the OSS had a tough time selling the establishment on their value and initially ended up working under

British supervision.

One of the OSS's greatest successes was the infiltration of Germany itself. Within a year of setting up in London, they had dispatched 150 operatives into the heart of Hitler's Reich, providing an invaluable intelligence network that stayed surprisingly well hidden. 95% of its operatives survived the war.

The OSS was also active in Asia, where it provided military training for anti-Japanese guerrillas in occupied territory. This included training the Chinese armies, which were in constant action against the invading Japanese throughout the war, as well as Vietnamese forces that would later become America's opponents during the Vietnam War.

Backroom Work

Equipping agents for field work was a vital part of covert operations. From seemingly mundane items like suitable clothes to the latest experimental gadgets, everything mattered to the mission and everything was thought through carefully.

One important area of work was the refinement of explosives. Timed fuses were extremely variable to start with, and a lot of effort was put into ensuring that a 10-minute fuse would actually trigger after 10 minutes, rather than four or five minutes. This was done through studying fuses and ensuring quality control at the manufacturing plants. Researchers also carried out experiments as to how much of which kind of explosive would be needed to destroy train tracks. Genuine French and German tracks, obtained by the army, were used in testing. At the same time, keeping secret documents out of enemy hands was very important, so inventors made cases that were hard to break into and which would destroy their contents if interfered with.

Ingenuity could be applied to seemingly frivolous inventions. For example, a paste was invented that etched the surface of glass so that agents could mark shop windows with rude messages about Hitler. And in addition to inventing new materials, equipment teams also had to learn to modify existing ones. Explosives were disguised as coal, skittles, and even turnips so they could be hidden from the enemy, while grenades were concealed in fake logs and canned food. Imitations of certain types of rocks from specific areas of France were made to be left on the roads, concealing devices that would burst the tires of German vehicles.

In order to blend in, the agents needed clothing that matched those in the countries to which they were going. Initially, the SOE hired people to collect these clothes from refugees in those countries, trading new British clothes for the battered ones they had brought from abroad. Later, they began to manufacture imitations, creating suits and shirts in foreign styles. Details such as seams, labels, and how buttons were sewn on had to be right, as did the shapes of the outfits.

On a continent suffering from war and occupation, few people had the resources to acquire new things, so suitcases, clothes, and even money were treated to make them look old and thus not draw attention to the agents who used them.

Both the OSS and SOE took great care to ensure their agents departed with complete, convincing, and coherent outfits. Every detail, down to the socks on their feet and the cigarettes in their pockets, had to match not just the country to which they were going, but their cover story as well. If their paperwork said they were factory workers from Bordeaux, everything about them had to match that story. OSS operatives were even taught how to smoke like Frenchmen after an agent gave himself away by casting aside an unfinished cigarette.

Forgers and secret print works produced the documents that would allow agents to pass safely through occupied Europe. Ration cards, travel papers, doctors' notes, and letters from grieving relatives about deaths in the family were all used to weave elaborate cover stories and the reasons why a person would be on the move.

Escape Operations

Some of the most ingenious equipment was created by organizations like MI9, MIS-X, and P/W&X. These were the departments responsible for helping prisoners of war escape captivity, and helping downed airmen to avoid capture. MI9 was the British group, while MIS-X and P/W&X were their American counterparts.

From early on, British prisoners were supported in their escape attempts by MI9, a covert branch of government. MI9 was the descendant of MI1, an intelligence body created late in the First World War to gather information from German POWs and British servicemen who escaped from captivity. It was primarily an information gathering organization rather than one leading escapes.

At the start of the Second World War, the neglected field of military intelligence suddenly became important again, and the idea of getting information from POWs was revived. Inspired by the accounts of escape attempts in the First World War, there was also an interest in supporting escapes by Allied troops this time around as well. With that in mind, Major J.C.F. Holland of Military Intelligence Research (MIR) proposed to the British government a new department that would combine these activities. MI9 would be given five tasks: to help escape attempts by British POWs, in order to return them to combat and force the enemy to invest resources in thwarting those attempts; to help escapees safely cross enemy territory; to collect information from returning POWs, both those captured by the British and those escapees returning to Britain; to prevent the enemy gaining this sort of information; and to support the morale of British POWs in Axis camps.

Holland's proposal was accepted by the Joint Intelligence Committee (JIC), and on the 23rd of December in 1939, MI9 was created. Major Norman Richard Crockatt, recommended for the post by Holland, was put in charge of the new organization. A 45-year-old veteran, he had proved his worth in the First World War, earning the Distinguished Service Order and the Military Cross. He was intelligent, organized, and willing to fight back when red tape threatened to stifle his work.

Crockatt

The work of helping men escape began before they even came close to captivity. MI9 trained servicemen in techniques for evading capture, and for escaping if they were caught. The pilots and crews of RAF planes were the focus of much of this training, as flights over enemy territory put them most at risk of capture. Training covered evading the enemy, too; if a man could avoid capture, all the better, and anyone who got out of the camps would need to know how to avoid ending up back inside. After 1940, this training was built on the experience of men who had evaded capture during the fall of France, including how to walk and dress to blend in while crossing the continent, who to approach for help, and how to behave once in contact with the resistance groups or escape lines set up to help Allied troops on the run.

In addition to training men for escapes, MI9 provided them with tools for the task. Much of the equipment was designed by Christopher Clayton Hutton, a particular ingenious inventor employed by the service. The focus was on hiding useful equipment so that it would not be taken from men when they were captured. Metal objects such as the ends of pens were magnetized so that they could be used as emergency compasses, and boot laces were used to conceal wire saws that could cut through metal. Handkerchiefs were printed with maps in invisible inks that would only become visible after they were laundered. Adapted clothing was a good way of equipping escapees. Compartments were hidden in the heels of boots. Uniforms were carefully crafted so that they could be easily transformed into civilian clothes, the better to blend in while on the run.

Hutton

Though they tried to equip men before they even became prisoners, MI9 also sent supplies to those on the inside. They marked packages with secret signs so that prisoners in the mailroom would know to distract guards from searching them. That said, Red Cross parcels were never used for smuggling, as the service that organization provided was too valuable to be risked by violating its neutrality.

For all the good work it did helping escapees, MI9 never lost sight of the goal embodied in its predecessor, MI1: information gathering. POWs could learn a lot about what was happening on the other side. From the tactics and technology used by the forces that captured them to rumors heard from guards inside the camps, former POWs were a mine of information for British military intelligence, and those who made it home to Britain were thoroughly debriefed. Meanwhile, coded communications were used to extract information from those still in the camps. Britain's edge in the air war was helped considerably by a radar expert who, from inside a prison camp, sent news of what he had seen of German technology.

Secret communications with prisoners mostly took place in two ways. One was through coded letters, many of them building on codes that husbands and wives had set up in case of capture. The other was through secret radio sets, either smuggled into the camps or built there by electronically savvy prisoners. By the end of the war, every prison camp for Allied officers had an illicit radio set hidden somewhere around the place, one of the most carefully guarded secrets in any camp.

The information MI9 gleaned went into furthering the war effort, and it also went into helping future escapes. After all, the experiences of successful escapees could be invaluable in briefing those who followed them, and all of this work contributed to improving and maintaining morale in the camps. The possibility of escape and the chance to get one over on the guards gave men hope and purpose. MI9 also helped with morale in other ways, such as providing news from home and ensuring a supply of care packages. Life behind the barbed wire would always be dangerous and frustrating, but with MI9's help, it at least became more bearable.

While MI9 and other governmental organizations helped Allied prisoners escape captivity in Europe, most could never have reached freedom without the help of the escape lines. The escape lines were part of the broader network of resistance that fought against the Nazis in occupied Europe. In particular, volunteers in France and the Low Countries provided hiding places, guidance, supplies, and transportation to escapees and those evading capture, keeping them out of the hands of the German authorities and providing them with a safe route home. For the sake of security, different parts of the lines often operated in isolation from each other. Fugitives were handed off from one group to the next as they crossed the country, seeking escape into neutral Switzerland or France or across the sea directly to Britain.

Routes into Spain were the most common. As a neutral country, Spain was meant to intern combatants found in its territory, and as a power that was sympathetic to the Nazis, Franco's government was happy to do this. Nonetheless, the foothills of the Pyrenees provided land routes to freedom, with plenty of hiding places along the way. Once in Spain, if escapees could reach a friendly consulate or British-held Gibraltar, then they were safely back on Allied ground.

There were several different lines in operation. One of the most significant was the PAT line. Established in 1940, it was run by a Belgian Army officer named Albert-Marie Guérisse, working under the name of Patrick O'Leary as a British Royal Navy officer. Working with MI9 and a range of volunteers on the continent, O'Leary created a network that could bring men safely across France to the Spanish border. There, they were smuggled into Spain by experts in the geography and operations of the border, many of them smugglers or opponents of Franco's far-right regime. It was difficult, dangerous work, and the man who ran these operatives, Vidal, was captured, tortured, and executed by the Germans in 1944.

A war sketch of Guérisse

Volunteers also acted as couriers and guides. They provided hiding places for the escapees, the most successful of which included brothels and seedy hotels, places where few questions would ever be asked. For a period in 1942, PAT escapees were evacuated directly from France by sea, using ships operating out of Gibraltar. This work was inspired by an existing operation set up by the Poles to extract their own men from France, and it successfully brought dozens of servicemen out.

Arrests and executions were constant threats for those working on the PAT line. Many volunteers were arrested during the line's operation; some were released, some were imprisoned until the end of the war, and others died in captivity. The work became more difficult and dangerous as the Germans tightened their grip on France, increasing security measures to stop the escapees, and things were made worse by traitors inside the operation. O'Leary and his companions operated in a world of shadows and deception, and it was nearly inevitable that some of those who excelled in this life would not be in it for the good of others. Harold Cole, a British sergeant working in France as part of the line, initially appeared to be a reliable courier, but then he blew PAT money on an extravagant lifestyle while failing to carry out his tasks. After being arrested by the Germans, he turned traitor, informing on other operatives. He was even released from captivity so that he could return to his work, now learning more information for the Nazis.

In 1943, a Frenchman named Roger Le Neveu joined the network. A spy for the Germans, he led several prominent members of the PAT line into traps, and most of the leading operatives were arrested. O'Leary was tortured but survived his imprisonment. In the end, both Cole and Le Neveu were killed during the liberation of France (Cole by French police and Le Neveu by the resistance).

Following the collapse of the PAT line, MI9 set up a new escape route by sea. Two MI9 agents were dropped into France, where they established a route from Paris to the Breton coast. There, escapees were picked up by boats and shipped across the Channel.

One of the MI9 operatives and several resistance members were lost to the Germans in the process of setting up the new line, but once established, it proved a great success. Codenamed SHELBURNE, it was used to ship downed airmen out of France through the first half of 1944, before being shut down as the D-Day invasion approached. The sea route was briefly reopened during the period between D-Day and the Allied liberation of Brittany to extract airmen and SAS personnel.

These escape lines were a huge help to Allied escapees on the run. Between 138 and 145 men were brought out by SHELBURNE. Another 98 were led across the Pyrenees by guides linked to the operation.

The PAT line was one of the war's greatest successes when it came to escapes, as it brought about 600 men to freedom, but this work came at a heavy price. Of the volunteers on the PAT line alone, more than 30 were killed by the Germans, one allegedly burned to death and some left mutilated by torture at the hands of the Gestapo. These were the risks of defying the Nazi regime, but they were risks brave women and men were willing to take.

It is harder to tell the story of officially sponsored escape activities for the Americans than for the British, because at the end of the war, the records of MIS-X, the primary American escape organization, were destroyed on the orders of a senior intelligence officer. But while there is less of a paper trail available to tell the story of MIS-X, there are still enough documents exist to piece together at least part of the story.

There were three significant organizations dedicated to the escape and evasion of American servicemen during the war. MIS-X was the most important and was similar to Britain's MI9. P/W&X acted purely in Europe, where it was responsible for assisting aircrew lost over the continent, acting with a more limited brief than MIS-X. The Air Ground Air Service (AGAS) was a significant subsidiary part of MIS-X, acting in the Far East. The origins of these organizations lay in a visit to England by Major General Carl Spaatz of the U.S. Air Force in early 1942. There he met Crockatt, the head of MI9, and was so impressed with what he learned that he sent Captain Robley E. Winfrey to learn all about the British organization. Meanwhile, British Air-Vice Marshal Charles Medhurst was sent to Washington to brief senior military and political figures about MI9. That summer, Spaatz set up P/W&X to liaise with MI9 and support the escape and evasion of his air crews. In October, the American Military Intelligence Division established MIS-X, with which P/W&X would also come to closely liaise.

Spaatz

MIS-X's mission was similar to that of MI9, which only made sense since it was based on that organization. It was to encourage and instruct American airmen and captured troops to make escapes, as well as instruct them on how to behave when captured and what their rights were as POWs. Moreover, escape equipment was to be prepared and distributed to air crews. Intelligence would be gathered, both from debriefed escapees and through secret communications with those still in prison. The Americans would liaise closely with MI9 in this work.

Five sub-sections made up MIS-X. The interrogation section debriefed escapees and questioned POWs in American hands, seeking information on the Axis war effort and the state of prison camps. The correspondence section maintained communications with the camps. The locations section identified the location of camps to make sure that the Air Force did not bomb them and evaluated information from the camps. The training and briefing section prepared troops likely to be captured, in particular air crews and certain Marine Corps units. The technical section designed, produced, and distributed escape kits.

Communications were achieved both through radio sets smuggled into or built in the camps, and through coded letters. These letters were often written in cooperation with the prisoners' relatives, in order to create convincing phony letters containing hidden information.

The inventors creating and distributing escape aids were just as ingenious as those at MI9. They magnetized razor blades to act as compasses, made millions of buttons containing hidden compasses, and hid a radio set in a cribbage board. Maps were concealed in decks of cards and table tennis paddles sent in aid parcels. Travel permits and ration cards were forged and smuggled in alongside German money to help men once they were on the run.

Most of this equipment was cunningly concealed to get it into the camps. On one occasion, a baseball manufacturer helped by making balls with spare parts for radios concealed inside. When the package was opened, a prisoner, informed ahead of time about the delivery, encouraged a guard in the mail room to join him in a game of catch, which ended with the ball flying over the wire and into the camp without further checks. For tools that were too big to be hidden, the parcels were marked with secret signs, so the prisoners could identify these packages and smuggle them out of the mail rooms before the guards checked them.

Like the British, American POWs organized themselves inside the camps, with the highest ranking officer in charge and others responsible for particular duties, such as laundry and food distribution. One of those reporting to the senior officer was the head of the escape and evasion committee (E&E). One example was Lieutenant-Colonel John H. Van Vliet, head of E&E in the Oflag 64 camp. Known as Big X, he kept escape activities secret from all the other officers except on a need-to-know basis, so that nothing could be revealed under interrogation. Even the members of his committee, each with their own areas of responsibility, did not know what the others were doing. They coordinated escapes, provided disguises and documents, spread useful information, and arranged diversions to distract the guards from escapes.

In 1943, the third American escape organization was established. Air Ground Aid Service (AGAS) was again based on the work of the British, who had been in the war longer and had established escape services sooner. AGAS was the part of MIS-X responsible for rescuing airmen downed in the fighting against Japan. Initially focused on China, their work expanded into Formosa (Taiwan) and Indochina. With the help of locals and Western missionaries, AGAS operatives helped in the escape of airmen shot down in bombing and supply runs, as well as a group of Marines who escaped from a prison train taking them to Shanghai.

Over the course of the war, around 12,000 American servicemen escaped or evaded capture. Over half of these came from Italian camps, thanks to the Americans' involvement in the fighting in North Africa and the subsequent invasion of Italy. A quarter of the prisoners escaped from Belgium and Germany. Just over a thousand came from the fighting in Asia, and only 218 of them from Japanese-occupied territory. Escape from Japanese prisons was far harder than from European ones, and the consequences of a failed escape were often more unpleasant, but in all theatres of the war, American personnel attempted to escape, evade, and distract enemy resources from the war effort.

Codes

Another vital part of supporting agents in the field was working with codes. Though radio operators kept their equipment hidden from the Germans, once a transmission was on the airwaves, it could be easily intercepted, and if it could be understood by the enemy, then the whole operation would be compromised. As a result, covert services developed an extensive system of codes and ciphers in an attempt to avoid this. In the early days, poems were often used as part of the ciphering process, by which words from a specific poem were used to create letter substitutions which could be undone by anyone who knew which poem had been used. At the start of the war, the British used published poems, but Leo Marks, the head of the deciphering section, realized these would make it easier for the Germans to crack the code if they were able to identify the poem being used. Instead, he commissioned and even wrote poems especially for SOE agents to be used in the encryption of their messages. These were later replaced by a more secure system of codes specifically created for each agent and printed on silk, which they could burn when they were done.

Coding often had to be done in a hurry or under difficult circumstances, with limited light and the tension that came from fear of capture. As such, mistakes could easily be made, rendering a message incomprehensible. The same applied at the other end, where tiredness and tension could lead to mistakes in decoding. Even atmospheric conditions could interfere with a transmission and garble a message to the point that it was difficult or even impossible to understand.

Everyone involved wanted to minimize the number of times a radio operator made contact, since each occasion inevitably increased the risk of capture, but if a message could not be deciphered, then vital intelligence might be lost. To remedy this, Marks brought in a system that ensured if a message wasn't decoded within 48 hours, the agent would code and transmit it again. His team would sometimes work around the clock for those 48 hours, desperately trying to understand the message and making sure it didn't have to be sent again. Past messages sent by agents and records from their training could be helpful, as they showed what sort of mistakes they often made.

In addition to the ciphering codes, agents were given checks, things they should include to prove they had not been captured by the Germans and forced to send messages. It was common to give them both a true and a false check, one they would tell the Germans about under interrogation so that it seemed as if they were cooperating, and one that was the real tell.

Vive la France

France was one of the biggest areas for covert activity, as its geographical proximity and familiar culture made it one of the easiest places to establish and support agents. Upon arriving in France, agents set up new lives. With the help of fake papers, cash supplies, and support from the local resistance, they found homes and took up jobs or studies in order to provide a cover story. They spoke and behaved like French people, for even the slightest slip, such as a word of English or a piece of clothing made in Britain, could lead to imprisonment, torture, and death.

Needless to say, life for agents in France was tense and dangerous. They relied upon hidden radios for contact with home, but as the war went on, the Germans got better at tracking these down. They would cut off power to parts of the town to see whether broadcasts stopped, allowing them to find the neighborhoods where radios were hidden, so operatives responded by finding other power sources, such as car batteries.

Radio operators spent their lives on the move. Some would carry their radios to transmit from different locations, so as to avoid leaving a trail back to where they were living. Others moved their homes every few days, finding shelter with families who were willing to risk their lives to resist the Germans. These families were told little about what was happening to minimize the risk of information reaching the Germans.

All operatives had to be constantly aware of their surroundings, and they used all the tricks they had been taught, whether it was spotting pursuers by looking at reflections in shop windows or looking back as well as right and left while crossing the road. Any time an agent left the house on a covert mission, he had to have a convincing cover story in case he was stopped and questioned. Random stops meant they also had to take care of what they carried. A gun might sound like a good idea for self-defense, but if found by the authorities, it would be a giveaway that the person was up to something.

Agents smuggled in weapons and other equipment for the resistance, and they also used them themselves, carrying out acts of sabotage, destroying important but poorly guarded positions, such as railway junctions and signal boxes. On one occasion, a team was smuggled in for the sole purpose of blowing up a fuel refinery at Les Telots. The mission was a success, but 5 of the 7 men were captured. The other two escaped by train into Vichy France and eventually made it home. It was one of the rare occasions when an agent had gone into France despite not being able to speak French and avoided detection by pretending to be a deaf-mute.

Violence became a feature of life for some agents. Though they had trained in combat techniques, many came from civilian backgrounds and had never been faced with the reality of killing before. Nonetheless, if they were detected and not outnumbered, then a knife or a gun was often the best solution. Many German soldiers disappeared while on guard or simply walking home in the quieter, more isolated corners of France. That said, escape was often a better option than fighting back, especially for agents who realized they were being tailed. Covert chases wound through the streets of big cities as they tried to shake off the men pursuing them without breaking into a run, thus giving it away that they had something to hide. Fast walks, winding streets, and crowded places were all of use when trying to lose a pursuer.

An agent with the right sort of job could be invaluable. A telephone engineer called in to repair broken phones in the offices of occupying authorities was able to steal papers, while intentionally doing a bad job on the repairs to ensure he would be able to return. A construction engineer called in to work on the defenses of the Normandy Coast provided details of what he had seen to the Allies. Claude de Baissac, the leader of one network, was caught with dubious papers and was saved from imprisonment by a police commissioner sympathetic to the cause.

Among the most useful operatives were prostitutes, recruited in the brothels of Paris. They used their position to extract information from the German officers visiting them. Some were spirited back and forth across the Channel so they could report on what they had learned, and while in Britain, they were equipped with custom-made lingerie to help in their work.

The Germans knew that a network of resistance fighters and Allied agents was at work in France, and they put huge efforts into tracking them down throughout the war. One method, especially in big cities, was to carry out random sweeps in which a group of people would be brought in, searched, and questioned for any signs of suspicious activities. Agents tried not to carry anything that might give them away, but there were times when it was unavoidable. Coded messages had to be hastily dropped or hidden when the authorities approached. This was one of the reasons so much care was taken not to carry anything English or American, as something as simple as an old bus ticket in a coat pocket could be a giveaway.

Train stations were a particular danger point. As passengers left the station, they were checked for identity papers, as well as their tickets. Random bag searches were also carried out at these bottlenecks. Rail travel was sometimes necessary, but it was also dangerous.

The presence of a wireless set was one of the biggest giveaways if the Germans raided a home. Blanche Charlet, a courier for a wireless operator, was arrested in the autumn of 1942 when the Germans raided a house and found the hastily hidden radio on which she had been encoding signals. She was imprisoned and repeatedly questioned as authorities looked for holes in her cover story that would allow them to prove her guilt and find out more information about the resistance. After escaping during a mass prison breakout at Castres, she went into hiding in a monastery and was eventually brought out of France by sea in April 1944.

The Germans became increasingly sophisticated in their efforts to find Allied agents, triggering cat and mouse games through the streets of France. Disguised secret police operatives would watch houses and hotels for days on end, tracking the comings and goings of inhabitants and following those they suspected of being enemy agents.

Directional radio tracking equipment, used to find secret radio sets, was transferred from military to civilian vehicles as the frames of civilian vehicles interfered less with the signals, making it less likely the vehicle would give away the authorities' approach. Once a rough location had been identified, officers in plain clothes with near-field detectors hidden up their sleeves would roam the area, narrowing down the location and unscrewing fuse boxes at likely houses to see if interrupting the power supply would interrupt the signal.

Captured agents were interrogated and tortured to find out more about their activities and contacts. Knowing that this was likely, agents were equipped with cyanide capsules before they went into France. If captured, they could swallow the capsule, ending their lives and avoiding a long, painful death and the possibility of giving away their comrades. Jean Holley, an agent based in Lyon, was captured without a cyanide pill and tried to hang himself, but he was stopped by his guards.

If the Germans captured a wireless operator, they used threats to try to get them to hand over verification codes or even to send transmissions for their captors. These messages started out as simple, unimportant things, like asking for more supplies, to ensure the trust of those running the agents in Britain. Later, they might request more useful resources or sit back and wait for more information. Over time, intelligence would fall into German hands, which led to the capture of several agents and the infiltration or destruction of resistance rings.

Commando Raids

The Norwegian Heavy Water Sabotage Operations

Acts of sabotage were an essential part of covert operations. Some were minor actions designed to inconvenience the enemy which could be carried out by local operatives, but others, like the attack on the Les Telots fuel plant, needed a more focused effort with specific agents sent in. Some, designed to take out strategically critical facilities, needed full-scale commando raids.

In February 1942, the Allies discovered the Germans had ordered the increase in production of water rich in deuterium oxide at the Norsk Hydro plant at Vemork in Norway. Known as heavy water, this material is valuable in the production of nuclear energy. Believing this indicated the Germans were developing an atomic bomb, the Allies decided they needed to take out the Vemork facility, so on the 18th of October, the SOE dropped four Norwegian operatives onto the Hardanger Plateau by parachute to carry out reconnaissance and preparations for the raid on the facility.

The Vermork plant in the 1930s

The original plan was for two gliders to bring in 34 British commandos, so the Norwegian agents assessed the ground and selected landing spots for the gliders. On the night of the 19th of November, they received a message that the commandos were coming. They set out lights at the landing point, but the gliders never arrived; thanks to poor weather conditions, they had been unable to find the landing ground and crashed. 23 men survived but were rounded up and killed by the Gestapo.

The Norwegian agents on the plateau spent months hungry and isolated, living off the land. Meanwhile, the plan for the mission had changed. A small group of Norwegian SOE agents were to be sent to carry out a more limited raid than in the original plan. They spent weeks preparing, using information gathered for the previous attempt to acquaint themselves with the layout of the heavy water facility.

After a false start in January, the SOE agents parachuted in on the night of the 16th of February, 1943, but the weather turned bad shortly after they had landed and they found themselves cut off by a storm in an isolated cabin. Days later, they emerged and finally met up with the reconnaissance group. They made their approach on the night of the 27th of February. Descending the gorge on the opposite side of the plant, they crossed the river below and climbed up the rock face to the railway line. There, they waited until after midnight to approach the plant during a change in guard shifts.

Upon reaching the plant, the agents cut their way through the outer gates but were unable to get through an inner door. The group split up, with some of them finding their way in through a cable tunnel and others by breaking a window, while a third group waited outside to provide covering fire if needed. Inside, they captured the Norwegian plant guard, planted their explosives, and set the triggers. They released the guard and everybody ran.

The demolition teams raced from the plant as the explosives went off. The agents had not destroyed the whole plant, as initially planned, but they had destroyed three months' worth of heavy water and badly damaged the facilities needed to produce it.

The agents met up with the covering group, re-crossed the gorge the way they had come in, and got away, crossing the border into neutral Sweden. Three weeks later, a member of the reconnaissance party was almost captured after he was lured into a German trap at their supply hut. He lost all but one of his pursuers in a cross-country ski chase, then killed the final man in a shootout and got away.

Early in 1944, the Germans moved their stocks of heavy water out of Norway on a ferry. Knut Haukelid, who had taken part in the previous raid, led a team to plant explosives on the boat transporting the water. When the boat sank, it took all of the German heavy water with it.

The Cockleshell Heroes

December 1942 saw one of the most celebrated commando actions of the war. On December 7, 12 British Royal Marines occupying six canoes were dropped off by a submarine along the west coast of France. They were to spend several nights rowing up the estuary to the port of Bordeaux, where they would use limpet mines to attack ships transporting vital raw materials for the German war effort. Afterward, they would scuttle their canoes and escape.

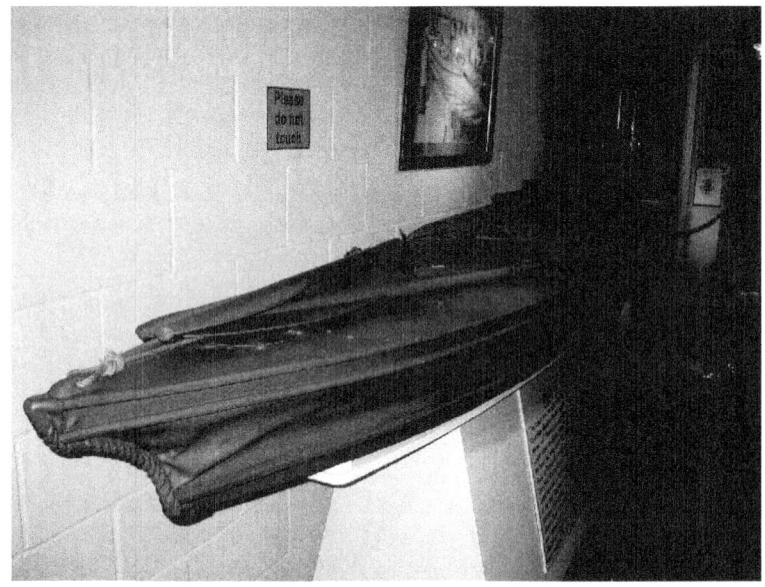

One of the original canoes

The men had spent the previous two months preparing for the raid. They had been trained in how to handle their canoes, how to use the explosives, and escape and evasion techniques for after the mission. They were even given information about how to contact the nearest POW escape line, information that was not normally shared for fear of putting operatives at risk. Their canoes were specially selected for transport by submarine and to carry all the equipment they needed.

One of the canoes was badly damaged during the launch and had to be abandoned. A second capsized in heavy waves, and the two marines who had been in it had to be helped by the other canoes before swimming to land.

A picture of the cockleshells

As they approached the river mouth, the commandos ran into a patrol of German frigates. They lay flat in their boats and paddled silently, hoping to get by them. One of the boats became separated from the rest, leaving only three, and the following day, while the commandos were hiding by the riverbanks, the crew of one of the canoes was captured.

The others didn't know what had happened except for the fact they were down to four men in two boats, and on the night of the 11th, they reached Bordeaux. The river was calm and the sky was clear, making it a good night to travel but also a good one for spotting approaching raiders. The commandos approached their targets around 9:00 p.m. and managed to lay their mines undetected, attaching them to six vessels before leaving the harbor on the ebb tide not long after midnight. Around 6:00 a.m., they beached their canoes, sank them, and split up, with each pair going their own way to find a safe route out of France.

The mission was a success - of the six ships attacked, one had been holed and later sank. The other five had been damaged and had to be heavily repaired. However, most of the commandos were eventually captured by the Germans. Though they were enemy combatants and in some cases caught in uniform, they were not given the protections offered by the Geneva Convention. In October, Hitler had sent out his infamous Commando Order, saying that any Allied commandos encountered by German forces should be killed. All 8 captured men were executed.

Only 2 of the men survived: Major Herbert Hasler, the leader of the expedition; and Bill Sparks, the man with whom he had shared a canoe. They walked 100 miles across the French countryside, avoiding German patrols before reaching the town of Ruffec. There, they found their information about how to contact the French resistance was inaccurate, but they still managed to contact a POW escape line with the help of the locals. After long weeks of hiding, they were smuggled across the Spanish border in March 1943, through rugged terrain where German patrols were sparse. Arriving at the British embassy in Barcelona, they were debriefed and then transported home.

Their escape was as remarkable an achievement as the attack itself.

The Balkans

In October 1940, Italy invaded Greece, and this initially unsuccessful campaign led to a German intervention that drove the Allies out and conquered both Greece and Yugoslavia by June 1941. A brutal guerrilla war followed as local partisans fought to drive the invaders out of the Balkans.

This region was important for access to the oilfields of both Romania and the Middle East, and because of this, the Allies were keen to support the resistance. Thus, both the OSS and SOE sent in operatives, but they found a far more difficult situation than in France. The resistance movements were bitterly divided along ideological and ethnic lines. In Yugoslavia, Croats, Serbs, and Slovenes fought each other as well as the Germans, while Greece descended into civil war between covert groups. Once a peace had been reached, the largest group tried to force its will upon the others. In Albania, there were over 50 different groups, some Nationalist, some Communist. The division between communists and nationalists was particularly important in Yugoslavia, where two leading movements emerged - the nationalist Chetniks, led by General Mihailović, and the Communist resistance, led by Josip Broz, commonly known as Marshal Tito. The Allies were already worried about what Europe might look like after the war, and about the spread of Communism in particular, so they threw their backing behind the Chetniks, but Mihailović used the weapons they gave him to attack the Communist resistance as well as the Germans. In response, the Americans and the British shifted to supporting Tito in the hope of uniting the resistance against the invaders.

Tito

The passions roused in the Balkans led to a particularly brutal and bitter war. Prisoners, whether from the occupiers or opposing resistance groups, were regularly beaten and killed. Even OSS and SOE officers were caught up in the internecine struggles, often asked to help one side or targeted for attacks by another.

Following the Axis invasion of the Balkans, many locals had taken to the hills. As a result, the role of OSS and SOE operatives was quite different from in France. Rather than living undercover in areas heavily patrolled by the enemy, acting as spies, and making careful, furtive connections, they joined guerrilla bands living in out-of-the-way villages, often in the high hills. From there, they encouraged and supported campaigns of sabotage and ambush against the Germans, doing their best to direct strong-willed local leaders.

The ability of Western operatives to direct guerrilla activities was helped by the resources they brought. They could arrange Allied air drops, bringing in weapons, ammunition, and other supplies for the partisans. This made them valuable assets for both Nationalist and Communist leaders.

OSS and SOE operatives often arrived in the region with specific objectives, such as destroying strategically important bridges, blocking the Danube River, or disrupting copper mining in Serbia. Though they might bring with them the equipment and skilled specialists to carry out the tasks, they usually tried to encourage local resistance groups to do the work. The idea was to stir up trouble and encourage guerrilla warfare, not for the Western Allies to fight their own Balkan campaign.

As in France, attacks on Axis facilities and troops often led to brutal reprisals. Captured resistance and Allied operatives were tortured and executed. Civilians in the areas near attacks were also rounded up at random and killed to discourage support for the resistance.

Captain Julian Amery, an agent in Albania, raised his own strike force from an unusual source. A group of several hundred soldiers had defected from the Soviet Union to the Germans, who had sent them to Albania, but the German commanders didn't trust the troops and they sat idle, feeling neglected. Amery convinced them to kill their German officers and defect again, this time joining him. Despite barely having enough shared language for even the simplest of conversations, he had won their trust and led them in a series of attacks against the Germans.

The invasion of Italy in 1943 provided a boost for the guerrillas in the Balkans. The Italian government had quit the war, and while half of Italy had remained in German hands under a puppet government initially led by Mussolini, the Germans could no longer rely on Italian troops. The Germans hurried to round up Italians stationed in the Balkans, meaning that both the Italians and the Germans dealing with them had been removed from the equation. Some Italians handed over their weapons and equipment to the partisans, and an OSS officer helped with negotiations at Split that led to a major handover of supplies to Tito's forces.

One of the most daring operations in the Balkans was the kidnapping of General Heinrich Kreipe, the commander of the German garrison on the island of Crete, in February 1944. A raiding party, led by Major Patrick Leigh-Former, was parachuted onto the island, where they met up with Cretan partisans and spent several days observing the general's routines, working out when the best opportunity to capture him would be.

Kreipe

A picture of the abduction team

Disguising themselves as German soldiers, they set up a roadblock on Kreipe's route home, hiding partisans away from the road. When the general's car stopped at the roadblock, they asked to see his papers, taking the opportunity to ensure the right man was in the car. Then, they dragged his driver out, seized the general at gunpoint, and drove off with him. The official pennants on the car helped them make their getaway, allowing them to drive straight through another roadblock.

The raiding party wanted to avoid bringing German retribution down upon the locals. To that end, they left a note behind claiming the whole operation had been carried out without Cretan assistance, but the Germans believed the locals must have known what had happened to the general and threatened to destroy entire villages if he wasn't found. Though hundreds of locals knew what had happened, none gave the information up.

Asian Operations

As the Japanese swept across Asia, the retreating Allies looked for ways to keep up the fight. In Malaya and Burma, agents had been left behind to stir resistance behind enemy lines, building up anti-Japanese operations from the safety of the jungle. In China, the OSS helped both Nationalists and Communists in resisting the Japanese.

In Malaya and Burma, British "left behind" teams often worked in small groups, using bombs, grenades, and guns to ambush Japanese supply trucks traveling through the jungle at night. An attack might last less than a minute, a sudden burst of violence meant as much to intimidate the Japanese as to do material harm, breed paranoia, and force them to behave more cautiously. The teams spent far more time trekking through the jungle to their targets than attacking them, but when they did strike, the shock value was impressive.

One of the most famous formations involved in this was Detachment 101, the creation of American General "Vinegar Joe" Stilwell. Led by Carl Eifler, operatives from Detachment 101 lived in the jungle, suffering through torrential rains, malaria, and supply shortages to carry out guerrilla warfare against the Japanese. They recruited local Kachin and Karen people to form a force of 10,000 fighters, and these rebels persistently harassed the Japanese, launching quick strikes before retreating into the jungle. The occupiers' punitive actions created further resentment against them, encouraging ever greater resistance.

Stilwell

Detachment 101 built up a remarkable operation behind enemy lines. Natives were recruited and trained and intelligence was gathered. Four airfields were built and kept hidden from the Japanese to ship men and supplies in and out of the jungle.

As the Allied presence behind Japanese lines grew, so did the operations. Together with local recruits, they ambushed Japanese patrols and raided their camps. To keep the jungle units supplied, Allied planes flew over and dropped supplies by parachute.

The OSS and SOE also sent operatives to train and coordinate with Chinese guerrilla groups, which proved far more challenging than working with resistance organizations in Europe. The linguistic and cultural barriers between the European agents and the people with whom they were working caused several problems, and the Westerners found the culture and the environment of fierce political debate common in Chinese groups alienating. With limited knowledge of local languages, they struggled to understand and communicate with most of the people they met, and everything had to be filtered through Chinese leaders.

Many of the Chinese commanders were unwilling to be led by the American and British agendas and would avoid carrying out suggested operations for fear of bringing down the wrath of the Japanese by providing only limited intelligence reports. They did not want to openly oppose the outsiders who were a valuable source of weapons and other equipment, so they told the agents what they thought they wanted to hear, including stories of successes on fighting fronts where little real action was happening.

Work with the Chinese resistance was frustrating but important work, given China's leading role in fighting the Japanese. Despite the difficulties, they launched ambushes against Japanese troops, sabotaged transport lines, and raided enemy bases. One of the biggest and last successes for these groups came in August 1945. Led by OSS operatives, Chinese guerrillas planted explosive charges on the mile-long bridge over the Hwang-Ho River and blew up two of the bridge's spans just as a Japanese troop train was crossing. The bridge was destroyed and the train fell into the river, taking 2,000 soldiers with it.

As was the case in Europe, both sides recruited spies to gather information on the other's activities. Very few British or American operatives were able to pass as natives and so they relied on recruiting local agents. Women played a particularly prominent role, as the Japanese recruited local women to spend time with Allied troops to get them to reveal information about themselves and their work. The Allies did the same, targeting prostitutes and mistresses of Japanese officers for recruitment. As with similar operations in Europe, the hope was that sex appeal might loosen the men's lips.

As well as gathering information, the Allies tried to spread misinformation to undermine Japanese morale, which became particularly important near the end of the war. The Allies were winning, but Japanese military culture made surrender unacceptable, and many soldiers fought on to the bitter end, which promised to drag out the war. To undermine this attitude, the OSS created false Japanese paperwork in the form of an order making it acceptable for soldiers to surrender in difficult circumstances. This was made using official Japanese paperwork materials captured in Burma with the help of a disillusioned Japanese officer. Detachment 101 got the fake orders into Japanese hands by planting them in a Japanese courier's mailbag after they ambushed and killed him.

By 1945, every facet of OSS and SOE operations in Asia had improved from its tentative start. During the last eight months of the war, OSS teams did huge damage to Japanese supplies and communication lines through acts of sabotage, and the killing of 12,348 Japanese soldiers, leaving the enemy constantly on edge.

D-Day

D-Day is the one event of World War II that all nations attach utmost significance to. Today it is remembered for spelling the beginning of the end for Nazi Germany, but it was the most complex war-time operation ever executed, and Supreme Commander Dwight D. Eisenhower himself was aware there was a high probability that the invasion would be defeated, which would set the Allies back at least a year in Western Europe if not longer.

To put the difficulties the Allies faced into context, the Normandy invasion was the first successful opposed landings across the English Channel in over eight centuries. Strategically, the campaign led to the loss of the German position in most of France and the secure establishment of a new major front. In a wider context, the Normandy landings helped the Soviets on the Eastern front, who were facing the bulk of the German forces and, to a certain extent, contributed to the shortening of the conflict there.

Entering 1944, France, once a lightly defended area, used largely for the recuperation of German soldiers from the Eastern front, was now the focus of Allied and German attention, with feverish plans made for the region on both sides. Reinforcements flooded into Northern France while tacticians planned for the impending invasion and counter-attack. The speed with which Germany had reinforced and strengthened the region meant that the Allies were less than certain of the success of the invasion. Britain, weary of amphibious landings after the disastrous Expeditionary Force campaign of 1940 came perilously close complete obliteration, was more than anxious. Allied military fortunes had been, at best, mixed.

During the first half of 1944, the Americans and British began a massive buildup of men and resources in England, while the military leaders devised an enormous and complex amphibious invasion of Western Europe. Though the Allies theoretically had several different staging grounds for an attack on different sides of the continent, the most obvious place for an invasion was just across the English Channel from Britain into France. And though the Allies used misinformation to deceive the Germans, Hitler's men built an extensive network of coastal fortifications throughout France to protect against just such an invasion. Largely under the supervision of Rommel, the Germans constructed the "Atlantic Wall", across which reinforced concrete pillboxes for German defenders were built close to the beaches for infantry to use machine guns and anti-tank artillery. Large obstacles were placed along the beaches to effectively block tanks on the ground, while mines and underwater obstacles were planted to stop landing craft from getting close enough.

Britain, due to its limited size and manpower, had relied upon deception as a force multiplier. Churchill particularly understood the importance of deception, when at the "Big Three" Conference he said, "In wartime, truth is so precious that she should always be attended by a bodyguard of lies." The resulting *Operation Bodyguard* was the deception plan created for use with the Normandy invasion. The plan was to trick the Germans into thinking the expected invasion would come in late summer 1944, and would be accompanied by an invasion in

Norway, Greece and elsewhere in Europe. The goal was to trick the Germans into defending areas away from the invasion, thus posing less threat to the success of *Overlord*. On an operational level it hoped to disguise the strength, timing and objectives of the invasion.

A further element of *Bodyguard* was *Operation Fortitude*. *Fortitude* marked one of the most ambitious, successful deception plans in the history of warfare. *Fortitude* was divided into two parts, North and South. Both parts involved the creation of fake armies, one based in Edinburgh in the north and one on the south east coast of England which threatened Pas de Calais, the most obvious area of France for invasion. The Allies went to remarkable lengths to ensure the success of the operation. A fictional U.S. Army group under George Patton was created in the south. Every effort was made to ensure operational security while also allowing the Germans to see the dummy war material and supporting infrastructure to add weight to the ruse. Dummy invasion craft were constructed at ports, inflatable trucks and tanks lined the roads in Scotland and around Patton's fictional army group. Luftwaffe aircraft were allowed fly over the inflatable army while being kept far from the actual invasion preparations. The deception was reinforced by frantic radio signals emanating from *Fortitude* north and south to the amount expected from a large size invasion group.

Inflatable tank as part of Operation Bodyguard

A crucial factor to the success of Allied deception was the use of double agents. Successful espionage by I5 had turned all German agents in Britain to the Allied side by the launch of *Overlord*. By the beginning of 1944, MI5 had 15 agents feeding false information to the Germans, with just enough reliable information to maintain their credibility. The most celebrated was "Garbo," a Spanish agent who created a fictitious network of 24 spies while working as a double agent for the British. The benefits of having such a fictitious network of agents was Garbo could create an identity for his agents to best fit the information given to the Germans. Hitler was so certain of Garbo's loyalty and value that he awarded him the prestigious Iron Cross, a decoration normally reserved for military heroes.

Garbo

Garbo provided details about the fictional Calais operation, including a scheduled date that came after the real landings further west. Hitler moved valuable resources, including tank formations, to defend Calais. Even after the D-Day landings, Garbo maintained the illusion that Overlord was a feint and the real thing would be coming soon to Calais. Hitler withheld tough armored forces for vital weeks, undermining his efforts to throw back the Allies so he could defend Calais.

Ensuring the Germans took the bait was a far more difficult prospect than creating the misinformation in the first instance. By 1944, the Allies had a massive advantage in terms of intelligence with the cracking of German enigma codes. Allied deciphering of German codes was so successful by 1944 that those responsible literally could not keep up with the overflow of information. What the intelligence was showing was that the Germans, in the days preceding the invasion of Europe, still had no real idea when or where the invasion was to take place. To complement the allied deception effort, the Royal Air Force dropped twice as many bombs on the Pas de Calais than it did in Normandy in preparation for the invasion.

The operation's success can be seen in the length of time it took the Germans to realize it was deception, even after the landings of June 6. It was not until mid-July that the German High Command realized Patton's threat to Calais from southern England was over. Without *Fortitude*, the Germans would have had free reign to maximize its forces at the point of attack in Normandy and with it, it is unclear whether the Allied invasion would have succeeded. Against such a formidable foe, however, the Allies needed to rely on every trick in the book.

Thus, even as the Atlantic Wall was strengthened, *Operation Fortitude* tricked Hitler into keeping 13 divisions in Norway rather than reinforcing the Normandy peninsula. It had also tricked German High Command into believing that 89 Allied divisions were preparing to land, with enough landing craft to bring 20 divisions ashore. In actuality, the figures were 47 and 6 respectively. Overreliance on intelligence crippled German defensive efforts in Normandy; it would not have taken a genius commander to realize that an exhausted Britain and a U.S. Army fighting a multi-theatre war in the Pacific, Africa, Western Europe and Italy could not have fielded 87 divisions to attack Europe. Instead the Germans swallowed Allied misinformation hook, line and sinker. Statistics show the extent to which the German High Command were tricked by Allied deception plans. The Fifteenth Army, based at Pas de Calais, grew to a strength of 18 infantry and two panzer divisions. The Seventh Army, based in Normandy, had just 14 infantry and one panzer divisions. To make matters more complicated for the smaller force defending Normandy, the size of their theater of operations stretched for 995 miles of coastline. Rommel and von Rundstedt were both reminded of Frederick II's maxim, "He who defends everything, defends nothing."

In conjunction with planning in Britain, by June 1944, the French Resistance had grown to a movement of 100,000 men and women, all waiting for the opportunity to free their country. When D-Day came, they finally had their chance. The signal to go into action came from Radio London. Broadcasting from Britain, this French-language station was set up by the Free French to counter German propaganda, encourage resistance, and send covert messages to the resistance. Radio sets were too cumbersome and costly to be provided for all the resistance groups, as well as putting their owners at risk if the Nazi authorities found them, but no one stopped the French from having ordinary radio sets, and this was where Radio London's resistance role came in.

Radio London broadcasts included a section entitled "personal messages". These cryptic phrases would sound like nonsense to an outsider, though it was obvious even to the Germans they included coded messages, but knowing there were secret messages was not the same as understanding them. Resistance groups gave British authorities phrases to read out to signal certain events, such as the imminent arrival of a parachute supply drop. When included in the personal messages, these told resistance cells to get ready while giving almost nothing away to the Nazis.

As the invasion approached, the personal messages grew in number. The resistance was encouraged to attack German communications networks. Their sabotage, together with Allied bomber raids, crippled rail networks across northern France, destroying huge numbers of trains that could have been used to bring troops into action. Even to those outside the resistance, the volume of personal messages made it clear that something was coming.

Just as the invasion fleet had prepared to set out, Radio London broadcast its most critical message, the first stanza of Paul Verlaine's poem "Chanson d'automne". This told the resistance the invasion was to start within 24 hours, and a fresh burst of activity took hold. 577 railroads and 30 roads were destroyed, along with 32 telecommunications sites, impairing military transport and communications. Across France, resistance groups rose up in open revolt, attacking the Germans.

This would prove a tragic decision for some in the resistance. Far from the Allied landing zone, they were cut off and killed by the Germans long before help was able to arrive, but their efforts, and particularly the actions in Normandy, drew off Nazi forces, helping to make D-Day a success.

The resistance was encouraged and supported in their D-Day uprisings by a new form of Allied covert action group, the Jedburgh teams. The Jedburgh teams consisted of three men, one of them always French, each of them equipped with a radio set. Unlike most previous operatives the Allies had smuggled into France, they wore uniforms. Though their activities involved elements of evasion and covert warfare, they were marked as soldiers rather than spies.

These teams were a combined OSS and SEO effort, working with the Free French. Preparations including planning and recruiting over a year before D-Day, with most of the training taking place at Milton Hall near Peterborough. There, they went through rigorous physical training, rehearsed attacks on railway lines, airports, and factories, and learned how to signal planes in to land.

To many on the teams, it seemed those in command did not expect them to make it out of their dangerous missions alive, but they had no qualms about the work, understanding the crucial role they would play in the war. The orders given to the Jedburgh teams were to create as much disruption as possible behind enemy lines. Like the resistance, they would sabotage vehicles, blow up roads and railways, and generally stir up trouble to preoccupy and delay the Germans. They were not told about the wider strategic picture surrounding their activities. That way, if they were captured, they could not give important information away regarding Allied plans.

The first Jedburgh teams were dropped days before the invasion, with the rest following in its aftermath. In all, a total of 93 teams were scattered across France. Their first task was to bury their parachutes and contact the local resistance. This sometimes went smoothly, especially if there was an SOE operative in the area, but sometimes they had to improvise after their contacts didn't turn up.

Working with the resistance provided great opportunities. Local knowledge told them where best to attack the Germans, and local people gave them places to hide. Support from resistance fighters meant they had far more men than the groups of three in which they had arrived, but despite being officially brought under the Allied military command's wing, the resistance was not used to obeying orders. Some showed more enthusiasm than sense, leading to badly judged attacks in which men were killed and captured.

The Jedburgh teams and their resistance contacts launched a campaign of guerrilla warfare against German forces in France. They ambushed advancing troops and blocked roads, delaying enemy advances. As small groups in occupied territory, they lived the lives of outlaws, constantly running and hiding to avoid German patrols.

In addition to launching attacks, the Jedburgh teams gathered intelligence for the Allies. One Jedburgh operative, accompanied by a young man from the resistance, managed to avoid German patrols to sneak into the town of Nice at night to obtain maps and details of the port from the harbormaster. These became the basis for a report about Nice that was invaluable in their preparations to invade the south of France.

Germany's Covert Operations

Though the Americans and British led the way in covert warfare, both sides made use of such techniques, and the Germans had their own spies and commandos.

In March 1942, Hubert Lauwers, an SOE radio operator in the Netherlands, was captured by the Gestapo, and what followed was one of the most successful anti-infiltration operations of the war. Lauwers was questioned by Major Hermann Giskes, an agent of the Abwehr, the German military intelligence service. Clever and resourceful, Giskes recognized the opportunity to fulfill a long-held Abwehr ambition and turn the radio operator into a double agent in something they referred to as "Englandspiel" (the game against England). After a huge amount of persuasion, Giskes had convinced Lauwers that operating his radio on behalf of the Germans was the only way to save his life. Lauwers left out his security checks so that those receiving the message in Britain would know what had happened, but this somehow went unnoticed, so the SOE believed their radio operative was still in place.

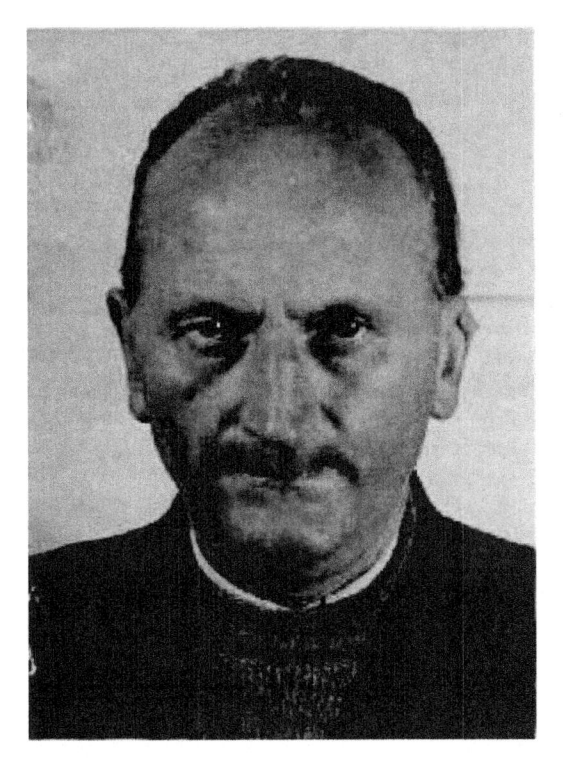

Giskes

Control of the radio set allowed the Germans to gather further intelligence and send false information. Over the next year and a half, they took control of the SOE operation in the Netherlands, turning a growing number of radios over to their cause. In total, 350 resistance operatives were arrested, 52 Allied agents were greeted by the Gestapo as soon as they reached the continent, and 350 containers of supplies were received by the Germans instead of the resistance, some of them being used to equip Germany's own covert commando forces.

After many months, Leo Marks, who had headed up the SOE's deciphering team, realized something was wrong, namely that the messages they had been receiving from the Netherlands had literally been too perfect. Since they lacked a single mistake, it was as if they were being encoded by professional cryptographers, not SOE agents who had been hastily trained in a wide range of skills. To test his theory, Marks sent a deliberately indecipherable message, one only a cryptographer could crack. When he received a reply instead of a request to send the message again, he became convinced the Germans were on the other end of the line.

Marks struggled to convince his superiors that the operation had been turned, and in late 1943, two agents escaped captivity in Holland and made it back to Britain. They told the SOE that the Dutch operation had been fatally compromised, but their account was undermined by a "resistance" message arranged by Giskes, saying the two were double agents sent by the Gestapo.

At last, most people in the SOE came around to Marks' view. Realizing it was over, Giskes sent one final, mocking message on April Fool's Day in 1944 before shutting the radios off: "To [SOE section chiefs] Messrs Blunt, Bingham and Succs Ltd., London. In the last time you are trying to make business in Netherlands without our assistance…we think this rather unfair in view of our long and successful co-operation as your sole agents…but never mind whenever you will come to pay a visit to the Continent you may be assured that you will be received with the same care and result as all those who you sent us before…so long." Giskes had achieved a great deal and felt he could let go in good humor.

During the first half of the war, the Germans lacked the commando units needed to carry out covert raids and sabotage missions. In 1942, Hitler decided to change this when he founded the Hunting Group, Germany's own commando corps, led by a veteran SS officer named Otto Skorzeny. A tall, scarred man with an air of arrogance, Skorzeny was smart, aggressive, and a dedicated Nazi, making him the ideal leader for the new unit. A trained engineer and decorated combatant, he had just the right mix of skills for sabotage and special operations. To carry out his missions, he recruited specialist soldiers from across the German Armed Forces. Struggling for resources, he used Giskes' corrupted Dutch resistance to obtain weapons from the British.

Skorzeny

In July 1943, Mussolini was overthrown and imprisoned by a new pro-Allied Italian government, and Hitler personally ordered Skorzeny to rescue him. Mussolini was held in an Apennine ski resort, and Skorzeny led the Hunting Group in a glider to land there. When his own glider crashed, he leapt out, assaulted the building in which Mussolini was being held, beat the guards, smashed a radio, and rescued the dictator. The getaway plane had been damaged during the landing, so Skorzeny and Mussolini had to be carried out in a spotter plane. Their combined weight so overburdened the small plane that paratroopers had to hold the wings up during take-off, but they got out and the mission was a success. Following that, high command gave him permission to expand his force and add new techniques, including frogmen and specialist torpedoes.

By October 1944, Hungarian dictator Admiral Miklós Horthy was starting to look unreliable, and to prevent Hungary from leaving the Axis side, Skorzeny and his men were sent into Budapest undercover. Seeing that Horthy was likely to abandon Germany, they kidnapped his son. In response, Horthy announced he was making peace with Russia and turning against the Germans.

Horthy

Through a mixture of diplomacy and deception, Skorzeny managed to take control of the Burgberg Castle, Horthy's headquarters, and capture the ageing leader. In his place, he installed a new pro-German ruler, keeping Hungary on Germany's side. The Hunting Group had changed the allegiance of a nation, a more important achievement than their highly praised Mussolini rescue.

In late 1944, as the Allies advanced across Europe, Hitler prepared a counterattack in the Ardennes. On his orders, Skorzeny came up with his grandest plan yet - he recruited 3,000 English-speaking soldiers, disguised as Allied troops, to cross enemy lines ahead of the attack, cut communications lines, and sow the seeds of confusion to hinder the Allied response.

This time, things didn't work as planned. The Allies quickly identified and captured most of the infiltrators, but the suspicion this caused became the biggest problem for the Allies, as they worried about whom they could trust. Men arrested their own officers, and General Eisenhower became virtually a prisoner out of fear for what might happen to him. Some of the Allies labeled Skorzeny the most dangerous man in Europe.

Despite this, the Ardennes advance soon failed. The Hunting Group re-joined the regular forces, desperately defending Germany. In the dying days of the war, some of them retreated to the Alps in the hope of fighting on, but when peace came, they surrendered.

Italian Infiltrators

The Allied invasion of Italy in 1943 was a serious blow for Nazi Germany. Their former ally had changed sides, and the Germans found themselves fighting against the Allies in mainland Italy. Though substantial effort had gone into repelling an Allied invasion, little had been done to prepare in the event the invasion succeeded.

The Germans rushed to find agents who could be sent into southern Italy, to provide intelligence from behind enemy lines. One option for crossing the lines was to disguise agents as shepherds. For millennia, flocks of sheep had been raised on the Italian highlands, roaming from one pasture to the next as the seasons passed. Agents were given simple disguises and flocks to guide and then try to cross the border under the guise of this migratory lifestyle. Others claimed to come from families who had been divided by the front lines of the war in Italy. It was an easier disguise to prepare and claims that these agents were traveling home to their families played on the sympathies of the guards.

To get these agents ready, the Germans set up training schools in Lombardy and Piedmont in northern Italy. Scores of volunteers were hurriedly provided with training and equipment, but they worked in a rush and lacked the experience the Allies had developed in their agent support services. The German training camps also lacked the attention to detail that saw the Allies use old clothing and equipment to ensure that operatives would be perfect fits for their roles. Spies heading across the border were given standard-issue briefcases and revolvers. After a few had been caught, the Allies began to recognize the briefcases and stop anyone carrying one. The presence of a matching revolver provided confirmation that the bearer was a spy.

As was the case in France, prostitutes became valuable intelligence assets for both sides due to the tendency of clients to let down their guard. In Aquila, east of Rome, a prostitute named Nadia Bufarina betrayed British escapees and the local POW escape lines to the Germans. When the Allies took Aquila, Nadia was, in turn, betrayed by her colleague, Gina, who had sold her out to the invaders, letting them learn about the Germans she had met. For Gina, it was the chance for revenge after having been forced into prostitution by the Germans.

To counter the German effort, the Allies had set up a three-layered system to track down agents. Field Security sections oversaw sectors immediately behind the frontline, which they patrolled in search of suspicious travelers, using roadblocks and detaining anyone without appropriate paperwork. More complicated cases were passed to Counter-Intelligence units who interrogated suspected agents. Their aim was not just to capture German spies but to convince them to change sides, converting them into double agents who would report false information to the Germans. Particularly difficult suspects went to the Combined Service Detailed Interrogation Centre, which featured specialized interrogators.

Thanks to the weakness of German preparation and the Allied counter-measures, attempts to infiltrate Italy ended mostly in failure. All 15 students from one German training class were captured and recorded in a mocking reunion photograph. SS General Wolff, head of Axis security troops in Italy, believed he was running 7 teams of agents, all of them providing reports by radio, when in reality all of the teams had been turned and were sending false information.

Rushed efforts had led to botched results.

Assassins and Politicians

The Allies did not balk at the use of assassination to deal with key enemy targets, and one of the most famous operations of the war was Operation Anthropoid, resulting in the assassination of Reinhard Heydrich.

Heydrich

A tall, rather slender individual with a long face, prominent, narrowly aquiline nose, and small, slightly squinting eyes, Reinhard Heydrich wore his blond hair slicked back and possessed some of the accomplishments of a "gentleman." An intelligent administrator and skilled pilot, the man nicknamed "the Blond Beast" also played the violin with notable virtuosity due to the fact that his parents were an opera singer and a pianist. Despite those innocuous sounding positions, young Heydrich received frequent, brutal beatings from his mother, echoing the extraordinary levels of parental violence inflicted on many psychopathic killers during their formative years.

Standing alongside such bloodstained figures as Heinrich Himmler, Adolf Eichmann, and Hitler himself as the architect of a series of mass murders equaled in history only by those of the communists, Reinhard Heydrich emerges as a paradoxical individual from the surviving records. The Blond Beast showed great devotion to his wife, Lina von Osten, and his four children, daughters Silke and Marte and sons Heider and Klaus. Nevertheless, though he appears to have been unusually troubled by the horrors inflicted on Jews and foreigners during the Third Reich, Heydrich applied his iron will to force himself to continue whenever a pang of doubt occurred. In fact, Hitler groomed Heydrich as his potential successor, deeming him to be a suitable Fuhrer in the event of his own death or incapacity. Heinrich Himmler, head of the SS, viewed his nominal subordinate with a mix of proprietary paternalism, awe, and alarm, recognizing him as a useful protégé, admiring his grim handiwork, and fearing that the ambitious and intelligent man would supplant him by turns.

Heydrich standing alongside Hitler and Himmler in Vienna in 1938

As head of the Gestapo, Heydrich constructed the infamous "Nacht und Nebel, or "Night and Fog," program. This secret police operation was designed to abduct (and usually murder) enemies of the state with such care and secrecy that they simply vanished, with nobody witnessing their arrest or their transport to places of imprisonment, torture, or execution. "Nacht und Nebel" was designed to sow deep fear in the German populace, a program of "disappearing" enemies carried out in as eerie and ghostly a fashion as possible in order to give the Gestapo the aura of a haunting, invisible, omnipresent danger which could strike anywhere without warning.

Heydrich also involved himself heavily with the seizure and deportation of Jews, though he did not oversee their actual extermination, a matter handled by Adolf Eichmann. The Blond Beast did, however, help to gel Nazi policy during the early war years at the Wannsee Conference on January 20th, 1942, the infamous meeting where the Nazis decided the fate of Europe's Jews. The Nazis sensed distantly they might be defeated in the war, so they wished to complete at least some "work" prior to that moment.

Hitler had appointed Heydrich "Reich Protector" of Czechoslovakia in late 1941, and once installed in his new post, the Gestapo chief set about conquering what was, in effect, his kingdom with a system he described as "whips and sugar," his own slant on the more familiar phrase "carrot and stick." Initially carrying out a number of political killings to show the Czechs he was not to be trifled with, Heydrich then treated his new subjects with a form of favor in order to win them over to the Nazi cause. In Poland, the Germans made themselves hated with their policy of random murder and grinding economic oppression, but Heydrich, by contrast, attempted to soothe the Czechs with high wages, good jobs, and various perquisites such as regular vacations in scenic areas for factory workers. At the same time, he left no doubt of the gruesome consequences of disobedience or rebellion. Heydrich was not exactly a kind master, but he attempted to create an unequal symbiosis which benefitted the Czechs as well – just not as much as it benefitted the Germans, of course.

As part of his program, Heydrich eschewed the trappings of security favored by most of his peers. Just as he had fearlessly confronted Russian fighters on the eastern front during the opening action of Operation Barbarossa, to the point of being shot down behind enemy lines and barely escaping with his life, now Heydrich defied potential death in a different fashion.

One of Heydrich's open air vehicles

The SOE and the Czechoslovakian government in exile under President Edvard Benes cooperated in creating the plan to kill Heydrich. The operation received the somewhat bizarre codename "Operation Anthropoid" and originated with the Czech exiles. The British government placed increasing pressure on these displaced officials to come up with a plan bolstering Czech resistance to Nazi occupation. Accordingly, in September 1941, the Czechs picked Heydrich as an assassination target, and the SOE assisted preparations.

Benes

Only the Third Reich's brutality provided some catalyst to resistance beyond the Czech norms of manipulating and passively resisting their conquerors. Nevertheless, many Czechs remained opposed to killing Heydrich outright, with good reason, as the event proved. Deciding to kill Heydrich from the safety of well-appointed quarters in England was a far different matter than facing the consequences of the assassination on the ground in Czechoslovakia, and as it happened, the Czech resistance, after helping to set up the Heydrich assassination scheme, made an 11th hour attempt to persuade the government in exile to abandon it.

The initial preparations for Operation Anthropoid commenced on October 2nd, 1941, seven months before they came to fruition, and the two men selected to carry out the actually killing were initially Josef Gabcik and Karel Svoboda. Svoboda did not remain on the roster long, however, due to an accident caused by a greatly accelerated timetable. While carrying out hasty parachute training, Gabcik and Svoboda met with near disaster when Svoboda struck his head on the ground during a botched jump and suffered severe injuries. Though they eventually healed, the injuries kept him out of Operation Anthropoid.

With Svoboda out of commission, the British substituted Jan Kubis, and training recommenced in Scotland. The two Czechs received thorough training in throwing grenades and bombs, firing various weapons (including Sten and Bren guns and Colt pistols), and parachuting. They also learned how to build and rig what are today referred to as IEDs (improvised explosive devices) but at the time fell under the umbrella term "booby traps." The third phase of their training featured orienteering in unfamiliar terrain, driving skills for a wide variety of military and civilian vehicles, and the use of Morse code. At the same time, British agents prepared extremely high quality false identification documents for the men, which even today remain almost indistinguishable from actual "Czech Protectorate" documents issued by the Nazi government.

Gabcik

Kubis

Under cover of darkness on the 28th of December, 1941, Gabčík and Kubiš parachuted out of a Halifax bomber and into Czechoslovakia. Thanks to anti-aircraft fire and bad weather, they missed the landing site by 50 miles. Though Gabčík was injured in the landing, the two men moved from safe house to safe house, spending as much time watching Heydrich's movements as possible. They noted his routes, his habits, and his typical schedule, and the Gestapo general's overall disdain for security also made itself evident during the months spent surreptitiously observing their quarry. Gabcik and Kubis grew convinced that two men could kill Heydrich, with a third acting as a spotter.

As the Czechs conducted reconnaissance, the local resistance leader, Bartos, an extremely sick man, anticipated the horrific consequences of the assassination and tried to dissuade the men from moving forward with Operation Anthropoid. The assassins initially kept their mission secret, but Bartos pieced the information together and confronted the men in April, just a month before the assassination took place. He begged them to reconsider in light of the massacres the Nazis would carry out to avenge Heydrich's death. Gabcik and Kubis met these demands with stony refusal and eventually stormed out in a rage.

While this squabbling went on, the Gestapo managed to intercept and translate part of the Czech transmission, warning them that the Czechs planned some kind of commando operation in the near future. One unknown factor is whether the British SOE would have called off the operation had they known the resistance's objections and the probability of compromised communications. However, Benes and his lieutenants did not inform the English of the communication or the doubts it contained, and SOE itself did not learn of the dispute until after the end of the war.

Either way, the Gestapo formed a clear picture of rising Czech "terrorism," and Himmler himself grew alarmed enough to visit Prague on May 1st, slightly more than three weeks before Heydrich's assassination. The Gestapo noted large numbers of commandos and saboteurs, as well as the capture of explosives, booby-trapped telephones which exploded when a person lifted the receiver, and so on. Himmler asked Heydrich to improve the security situation in the light of these developments, but Heydrich still refused to use a personal escort.

The Anthropoid assassins received a final impetus to act from Heydrich's schedule; when Hitler called for the Gestapo general to return to Berlin on May 27th, 1942, the men knew this might be their last opportunity. Accordingly, they chose a killing ground suited to their purposes. Along the road from his castle to Prague, Heydrich drove down a hill to the Troja bridge in the Holešovice suburb, and at the bottom of the hill, the road went around an extreme hairpin turn, forcing all cars to slow to a crawl for several seconds to avoid skidding off the road. Moreover, a tram stop nearby provided the men with an excuse to loiter in the area without drawing unwanted attention, and no police stations or Gestapo barracks stood nearby. The plan was to kill Heydrich, either with a burst of fire from a Sten gun or with a hand grenade, then escape to nearby safe houses using bicycles.

Heydrich and the men planning to kill him both woke up to a beautiful morning on May 27, 1942. This was to be Heydrich's last day in Czechoslovakia for some time at least, and, apparently savoring a moment of pleasurable sentimentality, the Blond Beast abandoned his usual clockwork routine and driven punctuality. Instead, after rising at the Lower Castle in Panenské Břežany, he ate a leisurely breakfast, which only ended at around 9:00 in the morning.

Heydrich, his mind no doubt far removed from the scenes of horror for which he bore considerable responsibility, enjoyed an hour relaxing with his family before he finally climbed into his black Mercedes touring car. The car's open top allowed ample fresh air and sunlight, but it also exposed the occupants to bullets, grenades, and even such simple weapons as thrown rocks or roofing tiles. Only two men sat in the car: Heydrich, in the back seat, and his driver, Oberscharfuhrer (Staff Sergeant) Johannes Klein, in the driver's seat. Both were large men, with Heydrich standing 6 feet 3 inches tall and weighing 206 pounds, and Klein around 6' tall and likely outweighing his commander. While Heydrich remained lean and agile despite his size, Klein's burliness made him clumsy and slow, though extremely strong. No escort accompanied the car as it rolled out of the castle gates past saluting sentries in the crisp uniform of the SS. Klein threw the car into gear and stepped on the gas pedal, speeding off in the direction of

Prague along a route he had driven dozens if not hundreds of times before.

While Heydrich enjoyed a leisurely morning, the assassins found themselves in an agony of suspense while awaiting their target. Indeed, they almost abandoned their vigil for fear of being caught, and their worry about being noticed loitering around the Gestapo chief's route was no idle fear. Another assassin, from a very different source, had met a hideous fate just a few weeks before thanks to a chance discovery.

In contrast to their reprehensibly sloppy behavior during the five months leading up to this moment, Gabcik and Kubis acted methodically on the morning of the assassination attempt, and Josef Valcik accompanied them as a spotter. The men carried their weapons inside a pair of briefcases.

Valcik

The men took a tram to the suburb where they had left their bicycles, retrieved them, and pedaled onward to Liben, where they took up their positions at the hairpin curve chosen as the ambush site. Valcik moved up the hill to a prearranged observation point, where he waited with his shaving mirror in his pocket to flash a signal to his comrades when he spotted the sleek black Mercedes convertible approaching.

Gabcik assembled his Sten gun underneath a light-colored raincoat he had brought for this purpose, then lurked as unobtrusively as possible near the tram stop as if he was waiting for one. Kubis, with his two grenades, stood on the opposite side of the street in the shade of a clump of trees, again trying to avoid drawing attention.

The three men positioned themselves for action by 9:00, but Heydrich, at that moment, was finishing his breakfast and walking out into the castle grounds to play with his sons. For the next 80 minutes, the three Czechs fidgeted, with their apprehension understandably growing as Heydrich failed to appear; after all, the longer they remained in one place and showing no interest in boarding the regular succession of trams or engaging in other normal business, the higher the chance that German police or Gestapo agents would spot them and move in for an arrest.

Finally, at 10:20 a.m. (some accounts say 10:32 or 10:35), Valcik spotted the black Mercedes 320-C convertible gliding down the street. A tram approached the hairpin turn from the opposite direction, but the assassins had already agreed that civilian casualties would be acceptable if necessary to carry out Heydrich's killing. Valcik pulled the shaving mirror from his pocket and flashed it in the sun in the direction of his comrades near the hairpin turn, and the two men saw the brilliant flash of sunlight off Valcik's mirror and prepared themselves for the moment of action.

As the Mercedes 320-C slowed to a walking pace to round the hairpin curve, Gabcik ran out onto the sidewalk, throwing aside the raincoat to level his Sten gun at the car and its two Nazi occupants. The Sten gun, a cheap 9mm submachine gun with a folding stock, featured a stamped metal build and a 32 round magazine. The British, whose long-standing gun control had thoroughly disarmed their populace and necessitated the importation of 5,000 donated firearms from the United States at the start of the war to provide the home guard with some kind of weaponry, had produced the Sten gun in vast numbers in an effort to arm their own forces and those of anti-Nazi insurgents throughout Europe.

The simple weapon, which fired pistol ammunition, seldom hit anything beyond 100 yards, but Gabcik stood just a few feet from his targets as he raised the Sten gun and squeezed the trigger. At this juncture, he learned another characteristic of the Sten: its tendency to stop working unless given constant maintenance to avoid a host of other problems and circumstances. Rather than a rattling burst of bullets shredding the two Nazis in front of him, the Czech heard only silence as he yanked frantically on the trigger. His Sten gun, brought so painstakingly to this point, was as useless as a toy.

At this moment, Heydrich and Klein each made a mistake that resulted in the Gestapo chief's death. Heydrich ordered his driver to stop, and Klein obeyed. Rather than accelerating out of the ambush, the aggressive Heydrich decided to capture or kill Gabcik, whom he incorrectly assumed was acting alone. Meanwhile, Kubis grabbed one of the anti-tank grenades out of his worn briefcase and sprinted out of the trees. The two Nazis, their attention focused on Gabcik, who still struggled futilely with his Sten gun a few feet away, would fail to notice the second attacker until it was too late.

Kubis acted decisively but clumsily. "He misjudged his throw. Instead of landing inside the Mercedes, it exploded against the rear wheel, throwing shrapnel back into Kubiš' face and shattering the windows of the tram which had stopped on the opposite side of the road. There were screams as the passengers were hit by shards of flying glass and metal. The car lurched violently and came to rest in the gutter, pouring smoke. Two SS jackets which had been folded on the back seat were whirled upwards by the blast and draped themselves over the trolley wire." (MacDonald, 2007, 153).

Pictures of the damaged car and tram

Despite the poor toss, Heydrich had suffered severe injuries in the blast, the worst being a large piece of shrapnel which ripped through his back and deep into his spleen. However, the Gestapo chief was so full of adrenaline that he didn't feel his injuries, and thinking he was unharmed, he jumped out of the car and staggered towards Gabcik, trying to get a clear shot with his 7.65mm pistol. Gabcik stood for several moments, staring stupefied at the tall, blond man in the black uniform stumbling towards him through the smoke and dust. Then, despite the shock of the explosion, the Czech made a stumbling run uphill. As he fled, the crack of pistol shots sounded behind him, and bullets whined past him. Desperately, he jumped behind a telephone pole and fired back at his black-garbed pursuer. Heydrich moved behind the damaged tram and returned fire, hoping to cripple or kill Gabcik.

Gabcik began to despair, knowing that SS men would arrive on the scene very soon. However, as the gunfight continued, Heydrich suddenly dropped to the ground; the pain from his wound suddenly struck him, and he writhed in agony for several moments. Gabcik, terrified, did not return to finish his target off but fled uphill, diving through the open door of a butcher shop up the road.

As that was going on, Klein pursued Kubis. The huge Nazi was slow-moving, but Kubis was scarcely faster. His forehead torn open by shrapnel from his own poorly-thrown grenade, the Czech assassin found it hard to flee with blood dripping into his eyes. He staggered to the place where the bicycles stood and leaped onto one, pedaling away frantically and leaving the raging Klein far behind him in a matter of moments.

Hitler responded with a characteristic lack of restraint when he learned of Heydrich's wounding at 12:45 p.m. on May 27: "Infuriated, the Fuhrer ordered the arrest and execution of 10,000 Czech hostages. […] German police collected all available evidence and concluded the attack must have been organized and prepared in England. Frank telephoned Hitler to confirm the British involvement and asked him to revoke the execution order, arguing that such unprecedented reprisals would be catastrophic for Czech morale." (Hauner, 2007, 85).

Despite the severity of his injuries, the mortally wounded Heydrich did not die shortly after the grenade seriously injured him. In fact, he lived for more than a week, dying eight days later on June 3rd at precisely the moment his relieved doctors believed he was about to make a full recovery. Two main theories as to his cause of death posit that he was killed by an infection, exacerbated by horsehair from the car's seat cushions carried into his wounds by the grenade fragments, or that botulism deliberately placed in the grenade by British SOE agents effected his demise. However, a third possibility – a lethal embolism caused by a postoperative blood clot – appears the most likely from evidence.

Predictably, the Germans responded furiously to the brazen attack on a high Nazi official, which included launching an immediate manhunt for the perpetrators. While Reinhard Heydrich's troubles were over, those of Czechoslovakia were only just beginning.

As news of the attack spread, ordinary Germans in the region grew enraged and began attacking Czechs, throwing bricks or firebombs into Czech stores and trying to kill Czechs they had lived alongside all their lives. The Gestapo and ordinary police protected the Czechs from this violence, which would lead to social disorder, but ultimately, the cruelty to be visited on the Czechoslovakian population would be officially organized, not a matter of vigilantism.

Meanwhile, the Third Reich offered a reward of 10 million Czech koruna ("crowns") for information leading to the hiding place of the assassins, and at the same time, the highest members of the Nazi hierarchy discussed what response to the assassination attempt would be most appropriate. Propaganda minister Joseph Goebbels voiced fear that assassinations would multiply if they did not offer an overwhelming response: "It is imperative that we get hold of the assassins. Then a tribunal should be held to deal with them and their accomplices. The background of the attack is not yet clear. But it is revealing that London reported on the attack very early on. We must be clear that such an attack could set a precedent if we do not counter it with the most brutal of means."

Eventually, an anonymous letter arrived at Gestapo headquarters, among 200 other letters, naming Gabcik and Kubis as the two men who killed Heydrich and pleading with the Nazis to stop killing people who had nothing to do with the assassination. A day later, the letter's writer, a

Sergeant Curda, walked into Gestapo headquarters and gave himself up. Stammering in acute terror, he gave the Germans the names of those involved in the plot. A parachutist himself and a brave soldier earlier in the war, Curda appears to have simply grown sick of the slaughter and believed that Benes' scheme to kill Heydrich was the act of a man detached from the real, actual horrors his decisions inflicted on the people of Czechoslovakia. Curda did not know where the assassins were hiding, but he was able to betray the location of several safe houses.

Finally, the Nazis discovered a Greek Orthodox preacher hid Gabčík, Kubiš, and five other resistance agents at the Karel Boromejsky Church. Having tracked Gabčík and Kubiš down in the church on the morning of the 18th of June, the Nazis attacked. The fighting lasted for two hours as the desperate agents held off their attackers. Kubiš and two others were killed, and Gabčík and the remaining men killed themselves to avoid capture.

The assassins were dead, but the reprisals were far from over. In fact, the fates of Gabcik and Kubis are largely overlooked in comparison to the mention of Lidice, the most notorious target of Nazi vengeance. The Gestapo and SS began a program of ruthless murder in Czechoslovakia which eventually left some 5,000 Czechs dead, and Lidice, considered a hotbed of resistance by the Nazis, would be completely destroyed.

Pictures of massacred victims at Lidice

A picture of Lidice in the wake of the Nazis' destruction of it

Out of the children given up for adoption, only 21 of the 102 survived. The other 81 were sent to Poland, crammed into a "gas van," and asphyxiated with exhaust fumes, a method so cruel that the SS and SD themselves eventually abandoned it due to the psychological shock caused by the sounds coming from inside the vans during the gassing process. The Germans exterminated another village on the day when the parachutists died in the church crypt, in revenge for the men's escape through suicide.

One of the Nazis' gas vans

Photographs still survive showing the ground littered with the corpses with Czech men executed by the Nazis during the revenge killings that followed. Guards drove bands of Jews out of their barracks in the concentration camps and gunned them down in reprisal for what the Nazis termed "a plot by the international Jewish conspiracy." Only with the coming of autumn did the killing abate, leaving a shocked and cowed Czechoslovakia in its wake.

Operation Anthropoid had taken out one of the leading Nazis, but at a terrible cost. Although the event is still well-known today, the assassination of Reinhard Heydrich failed to achieve the results desired by its architects. If anything, despite the careful planning and dramatic, spy-thriller appeal of the Czech patriots' doomed mission deep into the Third Reich, the scheme arguably caused far more harm than good. Just as Heydrich's death failed to impact the practical implementation of the Final Solution and other Nazi butchery, so it proved militarily insignificant. Heydrich's role was that of a secret police chief and mass murderer, and though he was recklessly brave in combat, Heydrich never commanded German armies, so his death made no military difference to the course of the war. The Third Reich's fighting machine remained the finest in the world at the time, though burdened by a factor ultimately proving to be its undoing: the incompetent, megalomaniac interference of Adolf Hitler in strategic planning.

Undermining the Enemy

Both the OSS and SOE were interested in destabilizing the Axis powers and supported schemes to undermine the Axis governments and even assassinate their leaders, though aside from Heydrich, these seldom came to anything. The OSS was particularly concerned with Hitler's psychological state and how they might undermine him, so they commissioned detailed reports analyzing his behavior and way of thinking. One of these correctly predicted Hitler's mental state toward the end of the war, with setbacks leaving him increasingly paranoid, unwilling to trust those around him, retreating into a safe space, and eventually committing suicide.

Inside Germany, the OSS networks gathered information on events around Hitler, his daily routines, and the security measures around him. Their contacts included not only Germany's underground political opposition, but also people inside the establishment, including a high-ranking foreign ministry official. They had heard about Hitler's increasingly strange behavior and the strain it had placed on senior officials within Germany.

Thus, analysts developed schemes to mentally unbalance Hitler, some of them more convincing than others. At one point, they considered dropping large quantities of pornography over Hitler's home with the hope that seeing the materials would somehow unsettle him.

Detailed plans were drawn up for assassinating Hitler and Himmler, his likely successor. It was believed that taking out the men at the top might critically weaken the German war effort and end the war sooner. However, the plans for these operations, titled Foxley and Foxley II, were never put into action. Indeed, the most noteworthy assassination attempts aimed at Hitler would come from disgruntled Nazis as the war turned against Germany.

Attempts to undermine the war effort were not all focused on the leadership. In 1944, the OSS and SOE started recruiting German soldiers who had been taken as prisoners of war and sending them back to Germany to spread rumors designed to undermine morale. These included stories of widespread infidelity by wives and girlfriends of soldiers away at the front, non-existent Allied covert operations in Germany, and a fictional order that only certain Axis units would be allowed to retreat if things went wrong.

The German empire was crumbling, and the OSS and SOE worked to ensure its collapse right up to the end, and once the war ended, many within the American and British governments called for their covert forces to be disbanded. In America, the FBI was keen to be rid of a potential competitor. In Britain, the Special Intelligence Service (SIS) had the same goal.

The leaders of the OSS recommended it be turned into a peacetime central intelligence agency, but they were overruled and the organization was disbanded in October 1945, with its intelligence gathering and analysis elements being transferred to the State Department.

In Britain, the SOE was officially merged with the SIS in January 1946, but in reality, the SOE was effectively disbanded. A month later, a mysterious fire in its records office destroyed the evidence documenting many of its wartime operations, activities a post-war British government might not have wanted to reveal.

Even as the hot war ended, a cold one was beginning. In March 1946, the British arrested a Soviet spy with knowledge of nuclear research for the first time, and SIS activities were stepped up. A year later, the Americans founded the Central Intelligence Agency, two years after disbanding what could have been its core.

Covert operations obviously played a crucial part in the Second World War, and while their impact is impossible to fully measure given their secretive nature and the fact that so much will likely remain forever shrouded in mystery, these operations impacted the world moving forward, and their tools and techniques were swiftly adopted for the Cold War.

Online Resources

Other books about World War II by Charles River Editors

Other books about World War II covert operations on Amazon

Further Reading

Henry Chancellor, Colditz: The Definitive History: The Untold Story of World War II's Great Escapes London: Hodder & Stoughton, 2001.

Flight to Freedom — The Colditz Glider — An excerpt from the Soaring magazine article on the Colditz Glider by Wade H. Nelson. Retrieved March 21, 2005.

Foot, M. R. D.; Langley, J. M. (24 May 1979). MI9 Escape and Evasion 1939–1945. The Bodley Head Ltd. ISBN 0-370-30086-6.

Holt, Thaddeus (2004). The Deceivers: Allied Military Deception in the Second World War. Scribner. ISBN 0-7432-5042-7.

Rankin, Nicholas (1 October 2008). Churchill's Wizards: The British Genius for Deception, 1914–1945. Faber and Faber. p. 466. ISBN 0-571-22195-5.

Reinhold Eggers, Colditz: The German Story Translated and edited by Howard Gee. London: Robert Hale, 1961.

Free Books by Charles River Editors

We have brand new titles available for free most days of the week. To see which of our titles are currently free, click on this link.

Discounted Books by Charles River Editors

We have titles at a discount price of just 99 cents everyday. To see which of our titles are currently 99 cents, click on this link.

Printed in Great Britain
by Amazon